52 Shabbat Musings

And Now A Few Thoughts From A Congregational President

By David B. Snyder

©2023 David B. Snyder

Copyright 2023 David B. Snyder

Foreword

As President of the Board of Trustees of Isaac M. Wise Temple in Cincinnati, it was my honor and privilege each week to sit on the bimah (pulpit) for Shabbat services. And I was also tasked with offering greetings each week. At first, those greetings consisted of the typical temple weekly announcements along with wishes for a Shabbat Shalom (Sabbath of peace). However, within a few months, that routine seemed a bit unnatural for me, as I often had a few other thoughts running around in my head from things happening in my world that particular week. And so

I started writing those thoughts down and they turned into the messages you are about to read. I would begin my greetings with whatever announcements there were, and then typically say, "And now a few thoughts," and then proceed to offer my message for that week. While my term was two years, what follows is a year's worth of my musings on Shabbat during my term, along with two extra messages offered on Yom Kippur, as the tradition in our congregation was for the President to offer a special message each Yom Kippur.

Some weeks these thoughts came easy to me, being written in a matter of minutes. Other weeks those thoughts were put to paper on a Monday and revised numerous times before Friday night in order to get the message just right. In all cases, it was not only cathartic, but also often therapeutic to take the thoughts in my mind, put them to paper, and offer them to our congregation. Now I'm not sure everyone appreciated the President of the congregation adding an extra minute or two to the Friday evening service, but enough congregants approached me over my term as President to say how much they enjoyed listening to my thoughts, that I felt it was a worthwhile exercise to publish them here.

So read one musing a week, or read them all at once! But as you re-read them, perhaps you'll notice that although the musing stays the same, you, the reader, have changed, and therefore the message may strike you differently each time you read that musing.

A few people to thank: Barry Snyder for guidance and for helping organize the publishing of this book; Lori Fenner, for proofreading and offering other suggestions; Marc Rossio for the cover design art; Michael Snyder for use of his photo of Plum Street Temple that appears on the cover; Rabbi Lewis Kamrass for his abiding patience as I offered these words each week, and for his suggestions on the Yom Kippur messages; and my wife, Jennifer Snyder, for listening intently each week and being my biggest fan.

These "musings" became a labor of love for me during my term and now that it has ended, I still find myself thinking about what I might offer each week, were I still sitting on the bimah…

I hope you enjoy them, and find meaning in them.

David B. Snyder

Table of Contents

Eternity Utters a Day	Page 1
All Shabbat	Page 6
Family Shabbat	Page 8
Must Have Balance	Page 11
Gratitude	Page 14
Post Pandemic	Page 17
Don't Talk Just Do	Page 19
New Year's Journey	Page 22
Better Future	Page 24
Mitzvah Goreret	Page 29
Blessing to Others	Page 32
Randomness	Page 36
Quiet Confidence	Page 40
Kindness	Page 44
Beauty in the World	Page 47
Craving Family	Page 50
Harry Chapin	Page 53
Expectations	Page 57
Jewish Commonality	Page 61

The Beatles	Page 65
Music in Me	Page 68
Laughter	Page 70
Christmas on Shabbat	Page 74
Extra Rewards	Page 78
Service to Others	Page 82
Love's in Need of Love Today	Page 85
Shabbat	Page 89
Country Music	Page 92
Making a Difference	Page 98
Connection to Action	Page 101
Not Alone	Page 104
Summer Camp	Page 108
Thankful at Temple	Page 113
Thankful Part 2	Page 117
Softball	Page 121
Brisket	Page 125
Laughter Part 2	Page 129
Passover – Rabbi Nachman	Page 133
Purim Lessons	Page 137
Be Happy	Page 142

Off to College	Page 146
One Year Difference	Page 150
Hometown Sports	Page 155
Volunteering	Page 158
Marriage Reconsecration	Page 162
Looking Back	Page 166
Breathe	Page 170
From Suffering to Blessing	Page 173
Significance	Page 176
Chazak	Page 181
Sacred Time	Page 184
Reflections on Two Years	Page 188
High Holy Days #1	Page 192
High Holy Days #2	Page 198

Eternity Utters A Day

There is a passage in our prayer book, Mishkah Tefilah. It is found directly before the Amidah in the Sabbath evening service. A poem from Abraham Joshua Heschel, that says the following:

A thought has blown the marketplace away
There is a song on the wind and joy in the trees
Shabbat arrives in the world
Scattering a song in the silence of the night:
Eternity utters a day

If you're interested, you can go to Spotify or You Tube and find a version of this set to music by Dan Nichols that will fill you up with the warmest feeling of Shabbat. Just search Eternity Utters a Day.

And it is this particular line that sticks with me. Eternity utters a day. What imagery that line creates. A peacefulness, a holiness so intense that it feels as if it lasts forever. Heschel wrote extensively about Shabbat and felt this almost mystical attachment and need for Shabbat – the need for peace that was the promise of Shabbat. To him, Shabbat was a day out of time, not a date, but an atmosphere. A day of

Eternity that offered the promise of a better world to come.

There are so many refugees seeking a better world - from Afghanistan, from Ukraine, and many other places. How is it that in the 21st century we continue to watch people's inhumanity to other people. We are so far away from Heschel's imagining of a world with Shabbat. How is it that peace is so far from our grasp?

We must use our value of tikkun olam, repairing the world, to do our own part, however small, to work towards a world of peace. The time is now for you to think about what you can do and how you can help. With war on our TV screens and in our news feeds, there is no time to wait. Start by building bridges instead of burning them – working with other people, despite differences of thought. Build on those relationships and then work for those that need our help most, to whom we can offer a glimpse of peace. Only by being a symbol of living a life of peace can we show others how. We must find a way back to Heschel's vision of Shabbat. And we should strive for peace not just on Shabbat but every day.

On this Shabbat, and every day, let us consider how it can be our responsibility, individually and collectively, to welcome the refugee, to help the stranger, to bridge gaps between enemies, to work toward peace, to repair our world, to make eternity utter a day.

Shabbat Shalom

All Shabbat

I have a book that I typically read daily – it is called Life's Daily Blessings by Rabbi Kerry Olitzky. For each day of the calendar year, there is a bit of Jewish text, or a quote from a Rabbi, past or present, or other Jewish figure, and then there are a few paragraphs of commentary about that quote or text. The one I read for today was from the Talmud and simply says, Yom Shekulo Shabbat, "A Day That is All Shabbat". This struck me, because the quote was so short, but even more so, because it is a simple message to remind us about the power of Shabbat, about the power of taking a break each week. I hope we can try to imagine days in the future that are entirely Shabbat – not burdened by the mundane.

As we head into the new year, I hope that each of you can find a way to make each Shabbat a day that is ALL Shabbat, that you can find a way to unwind, to detach and have a sacred day.

Shabbat Shalom

Family Shabbat

On this family night, where we were able to combine our young families Shabbat with our traditional Friday evening service, I offer these thoughts about family.

Judaism prioritizes the family. The commandments to be fruitful and multiply, to honor your father and your mother, to teach your children, are just some of our heritage that speak to the importance of our family units. And we mark so many occasions with our families – brit milah, bar/bat mitzvah, weddings, not to mention the holidays where family is of the utmost important –

lighting Shabbat candles together, the Passover seder and lighting the Chanukah menorah to name a few.

As we approach our High Holy Days, we can only hope this time of year provides another opportunity for our families to celebrate together, reflect together, pray together, and come to further appreciate the true value of family. We may be the people of the book, but I'd also argue that we are the people of mishpacha – of family. Or if you grew up in a certain era, you might have said, mishpoocha.

On this Shabbat, let us be ever mindful of how much we love our families, of the give and take, and effort we make to prioritize our families and how much we can live, learn and grow from them.

Shabbat Shalom.

Must Have Balance

In my personal reflection this High Holy Day season, I came across this concept from Moses Maimonides, the great Jewish rabbi and scholar from the 12th century: He said, that, "everyone should regard oneself throughout the years as exactly balanced between acquittal and guilt." Maimonides felt life in the middle, away from extremes, keeps us evenly balanced. It is what he and many others of that era referred to as the golden mean, a place where an individual can find tranquility and well being.

This is particularly meaningful at this time of the year as we each reflect on our lives over the past year and look toward the year to come. And it is becoming ever more difficult as so many parts of our lives seem to be pulled toward the extremes. While none of us are truly innocent and none of us are fully guilty, it is clear the concept of a golden mean offers us a way to find more happiness and satisfaction. I'll date myself here, but the 1984 movie The Karate Kid, also reminded us all that we must have balance. Mr. Miyagi and Maimonides seem to be of the same mind.

On this Shabbat, and into next year, as we continue the reflection and T'shuvah of this High Holy Day season, may we all find our own golden mean away from the extremes, and in doing so, achieve our own balance of tranquility and well being.

Shabbat Shalom

Gratitude

I have had a number of situations confront me this year that make me feel less than grateful and I have watched many others work through hardships where I am certain they, too, question feeling any gratitude.

And yet… ironically, gratitude may be the way out. Gratitude is defined as the expression of appreciation for what one has. All I read about those that practice this art of recognizing gratitude, is that it helps put things in perspective. Tragedy and hardship affect every person – it is unavoidable. But what we can control is our response to those tragedies and hardships. And the gift of gratitude is to reflect on what you DO have to give thanks for at any given point. Consider that there is always something for which to be grateful, something for which you can express some gratitude. This can be difficult for many of us – we can't simply flip a switch toward gratitude. Instead, I believe it is more of a process – like anything new we learn, it takes time and effort to change our mindsets. But what a better way to live – we can choose to give our hardships and tragedies their proper space in our world, give ourselves the proper space for grief and sadness, but train our brains to always reflect on what is good and positive in our lives. This is my challenge today, and I try to remind myself of the need to practice. And this is my challenge for you.

I'll leave you with one other quote I heard in a random interview about gratitude that struck a chord with me – it said: Gratitude taught me to love something I cannot change.

On this Shabbat, and moving forward, let us pause to reflect on the gifts in our lives, to express gratitude for those gifts, and allow that to propel us through our days.

Shabbat Shalom

Post Pandemic

We have spent an enormous amount of time and energy to fill our calendar with in person events. It all feels as though we are back in the groove. But are we? If the pandemic has taught us anything, it is that flexibility and the ability to shift quickly are the new name of the game. While we are so grateful to have so much regular programming back on the calendar, we must be ever cognizant of the need to be flexible in our fast changing world. For a large congregation, we have become very adept at this. Our rabbis and staff continue making things look easy as we move forward in this post pandemic phase. And we must be mindful of those in our congregation who may not be prepared for everything in person just yet. Which is why so many of our programs will continue to be offered in person and virtually. We continue to find ways to welcome all, no matter how they want to participate. That is the reality of Reform congregational life today and beyond.

On this Shabbat, may we look for ways to be inclusive and accepting, and allow that to energize us for the week ahead.

Shabbat Shalom

Don't Talk, Just Do

"Let your deeds sing your praise". I came across this quote and despite the simpleness of the statement, I realized there had to be more to it.

Let your deeds sing your praise. At first blush, it is a statement of ego. We should toot our own horns. And as we so often find, others are doing it, so why shouldn't we. It is human nature to want others to know about good things we have done and it is also human nature to constantly compare ourselves to others.

But there is a much deeper meaning here. It is not really our Jewish value to brag about things and to say, "look at me – look at what I've done." What is our Jewish value is to do good deeds and let them speak for themselves. Or more simply put, don't talk, just do. And perhaps that's what we should understand when we hear the words, "let your deeds sing your praises". We need to focus on the doing and find the meaning in the doing rather than receiving any praise for it.

There are so many opportunities we have right here at our temple that can make a difference for others. If you have never participated in any, I encourage you to start the new year by doing so. Do the deeds and then, privately, sing your own praise.

And so, on this Shabbat, and as we enter this new year, let us consider ways we can increase our good deeds. Not for the purpose of receiving praise but for the blessing of having done the deed.

Shabbat Shalom

New Year's Journey

Briefly tonight, here is a blessing I came across in my readings that is particularly applicable at the new year, like a personal mantra for anyone looking for guidance and purpose:

May your journey fill you with awareness, compassion, forgiveness and empathy, moving you to inner peace, wisdom and liberation from all that holds you back. Helping ourselves and each other along this journey, may we, together, relieve suffering, awaken new perceptions of what life might become, encourage self-realization, enlightenment and a strengthened

connection between thought, feeling and action.
Rabbi Nina Mizrahi

And so, on this Shabbat and throughout this year, may we all find purpose in our journey and find courage to take the steps to move past what holds us back. And in doing so, find a new realization of what our life might become and the impact we can have on others.

Shabbat Shalom

Better Future

So what are YOU streaming. For me, it's not a whole lot. But this past week I did start watching two shows – Peripheral on Amazon Prime and The Last of Us on HBO Max. Honestly, I'm not that into either of these – I am really just biding my time as I patiently wait for the return of Ted Lasso. But I digress…

If you're not familiar with Peripheral or The Last of Us, I'll simply tell you this, without providing any spoilers – they are both post apocalyptic stories and each paints this horrific picture of what life is like on earth in the not too distant future, and by not too distant, I'm talking about within the next 75 years. One talks about a pandemic fungus like a virus that overtakes the planet, and the other discusses how many events factored into the destruction of the planet including climate disaster, pandemic, war and others.

I'm particularly shocked by these two shows because I find it so hard to believe that within such a short time, our planet could even be in such a state. I know we have problems to fix – climate issues, political division, issues of race, gender and equality. But our history seems to indicate that when pushed up against a wall, we seem to find a way. And I'm not just talking about as Americans, but as a species.

Martin Luther King Jr. in one of his speeches said that, "the arc of the moral universe is long, but it bends toward justice." And while he was clearly taking about justice in a legal sense, I like to believe this statement has a more general meaning in that the arc of the universe eventually bends toward what is right for a peaceful planet, one of co-existence. But it is true that it does not bend on its own. People pull it towards the goal. This is an active process, not a passive one.

And so it is with our need to preserve our planet, our democracy, and all of our institutions, so that we don't end up in a world portrayed by these two shows. It is our responsibility to work towards a better planet. It is our obligation as parents to make this world livable for our children. And all it takes is a little effort, but effort nonetheless, and from all of us, to find solutions to these problems.

On this Shabbat, let us consider what our future should look like and do our own part to start bending the arc of the universe toward a better and more meaning future.

Shabbat Shalom

Mitzvah Goreret

You all know I loved my summer camp experience as I reference it often. And also my love for Jewish music. One of the old "classics" from my camp days popped into my head this week, and it is kind of an ear worm so it stuck with me. The song, called Mitzvah Goreret Mitzvah, written by Rabbi Andy Vogel, is a very simple song melodically with a simple bit of Hebrew that translates as: One mitzvah leads to another, one sin or transgression leads to another, and to be righteous is very good. This song offers some basic wisdom – do good and that will lead to other good deeds, and a warning that the opposite is true too – sin, and that could lead to other sins.

It was a great message to teach camp kids but one we can't ignore today. One mitzvah surely leads to another because the feeling of doing good for another person or for the community is so infectious – and I'm talking about the good meaning of infectious – not the COVID meaning! And once felt, you start to crave it - you start to seek it out more and more.

From soup kitchens, to providing clothing, to packing bags for kids in need, we have so many opportunities to make a difference in our community and in the lives of so many individuals.

On this Shabbat, let us remember our call of tikkun olam – to repair the world and seek out new ways to make a difference in the lives of others.

Shabbat Shalom

Blessing to Others

Here is a blessing written by Rabbi Naomi Levy that I came across and read on November 8th. Her blessing says this:

May God be with you, may health and strength sustain you. May nothing harm you, may wisdom and kindness enrich you. May you be a blessing to this world and may blessings surround you now and always.

As I read it, my only thought was that this was one of the nicest blessings I have ever heard. How incredibly kind and selfless to wish this for another person – listen again - May God be with you, may health and strength sustain you. May nothing harm you, may wisdom and kindness enrich you. May you be a blessing to this world and may blessings surround you now and always.

Of course, November 8th also happened to be our midterm election, further cementing the division and polarization that have truly engulfed our country. And I thought, how odd that I would read this blessing on this day. It is a reminder that we are so much better off when we can bless our fellow humankind, wish them health, wisdom and for other blessings to surround them. It is a reminder that, at our cores, we are more alike than not, that we all want similar things for ourselves, and our families.

I'm not sure we will find our way past the current political climate, but I certainly hope there is a path back to more civility and respect, and perhaps that path starts with remembering this blessing as a way to think about our family, friends, neighbors, and even those who may not think or believe as we do.

And so on this Shabbat, let us strive for the kindness that will allow us to ask for this blessing on others: May

God be with you, may health and strength sustain you. May nothing harm you, may wisdom and kindness enrich you. May you be a blessing to this world and may blessings surround you now and always.

Shabbat Shalom

Randomness

Our world keeps changing, sometimes in the blink of an eye, and then often, we have a reminder of our continual fight against hatred with what happened in Colleyville, Texas.

There is randomness that happens in our lives, and somehow, we are supposed to learn to go with the flow. And there is no road map to navigate on how to deal with these random acts and any randomness that may happen in your life.

I'm not sure whether to take comfort in that comment or not. On the one hand, it is a helpless feeling to think that random acts can change us so quickly and no road map exists to help us out. Yet on the other hand, there is some comfort in the fact that since there is no road map, there is also no right or wrong way to deal with these events. There is some freedom in knowing that each of us will have to internalize something and process it in our own way. Whether they be random acts of violence or random personal challenges, you get to decide what is best for you.

One important thing to remember is that regardless of your decisions, you have a support system in place right here at temple. I realize your family and friends will take a front seat in supporting you with whatever challenges face you or with processing emotional responses to what is happening in the world. But our Rabbis and staff and your entire temple community are here to help you work through these challenges as well.

So when these unexplainable and random acts occur, know that you are part of a caring community. You simply need to reach out and we are here.

On this Shabbat, and every Shabbat, may we be reminded of what is good in our world and may we be grateful for the blessings we have.

Shabbat Shalom

Quiet Confidence

From my book of daily blessings by Rabbi Kerry Olitzky, I read this passage from the book of Isaiah, "In quietness and confidence shall be your strength".

My immediate thought was how loud our world is. And it's not just our devices - our phones blaring videos and music, our TV's blaring streaming content, news and sports. It's also the people we see around us. We have reached a point where the louder you are, the better you are heard, and remarkably, the more credible you sound, regardless of whether or not you are. This is especially true with our politicians and the media covering our politicians. The louder they talk, the better their ratings. I used to think that the country truly lived in the political middle, and it was just the cable news that was espousing the extremes on either side. But that has changed over the past 10 years. Now, what they shout from their side has actually become the position of that side. The middle is shrinking, and most people seem to associate closer to an extreme than to the middle. How sad this is to me. And how different it would be if our politicians were required to follow Isaiah's advice. In quietness and confidence shall be your strength.

Just imagine a political arena where those campaigning and those in office simply put their heads down and got to work. I know that speeches are necessary. But quiet and confident speeches that have meaning and real content, not ones that simply speak ill of the other side. Our politics have always been contentious. I won't begrudge anyone who has a reason for and conviction in their position. But there was a time many of us can remember when issues could get resolved peaceably. Quiet and confident strength was actually an asset. We can only hope that moving forward, the memory of that time resurfaces.

On this Shabbat, let us heed Isaiah's advice in our lives, and practice what he preached. May quiet confidence be our strength and our mantra, as we try to build a better future.

Shabbat Shalom

Kindness

You may recall that two weeks ago, I stood here and talked about randomness in our lives and how best to process that randomness and react to it. And with that randomness there is comfort in knowing we are part of a caring community. So today, I reflect upon that caring community. In response to that randomness, I have witnessed some incredible kindness these past two weeks. Not just from our temple caring community, but from people I would not have expected. People are really quite nice, and I don't think we always take the time to appreciate that fact.

We are so quick to judge and so short tempered that we often never get to see the kindness of people. We see a social media post that reflects a different viewpoint than our own, and we immediately shut someone out. Perhaps we need to seek and be willing to accept the kindness of people first, and offer that kindness to others. If we believe different things, both sides start the relationship with a respect and kind spirit that makes it easier to engage with each other, even if there are differences of thought and opinion.

I think Anne Frank had it right. We are most familiar with the last line of this quote, but the full quote is: "It's really a wonder that I haven't dropped all my ideals, because they seem so absurd and impossible to carry out. Yet I keep them, because in spite of everything, I still believe that people are really good at heart." People ARE good at heart, and kindness exudes if only you look for it, and it will drive you to want to reciprocate.

On this Shabbat, may we look for ways to be kind and receive kindness to help nurture our own souls and the relationships we have with others.

Shabbat Shalom

Beauty in the World

I spent most of last week in Scottsdale, Arizona. I traveled there with an old camp friend so we could go hiking. We stayed at a very nice hotel, so it was luxury at night, but definitely rugged during the day. Over the course of three days we hiked over 15 very rocky and steep miles, and also climbed over 5000 feet. Each day was a different mountain hike and each day I stood on a mountaintop and surveyed the valley of the sun below me. It was breathtaking and exhilarating. Each day had its challenges – some steeper than others, and some difficult to simply hang on. But oh, so worth it when I reached the top. Even the photos and videos I took don't do justice to what my eyes saw standing there at each peak on each beautiful sunny day.

We spend so much of our days wrapped up with our careers, and mired in the daily news that tells us about politics, wars, disease, division, climate change and so many other stories that simply depress us and make us feel lousy about the world in which we live.

We just forget that, as the old saying goes, we need to stop and smell the roses. Our world is full of beauty and majesty. It's just that today, we sometimes need to be reminded of it and to go looking for it. And look I did. And it was very good.

On this Shabbat, let us try to actually rest and pull ourselves away from work and the news of the week, and take some time to admire the beauty in our world.

Shabbat Shalom

Craving Family

I'm not sure it's kosher to say this, but when it comes to Thanksgiving, I'm a pig at the dinner table. And it's never really been about the turkey for me, it's always been about the side dishes. Until more recent years, when my piggishness has extended to a desire for the turkey leg, something I never wanted as a kid, but something I do now as an homage to my grandfather, and because it's delicious!

This year was no different, but I found myself wanting to be gluttonous for more than food. This is my first year as an empty nester and having my kids home from college for the holiday has become more special as the times I get to see my boys will continue to gradually decrease as they move on in their lives. So I spent much time over the past forty eight hours craving quality time with them, and in a larger sense, quality time with my entire family. I am fortunate to have loving and welcoming relatives on both my side of the family and my wife's side of the family, that in a year such as this, we have to work to find time to spend with each group. But we find a way to make it work and as each year goes by, I find this as satisfying as any Thanksgiving meal.

On this holiday weekend, may you crave family and have the satisfaction of togetherness.

Shabbat Shalom

Harry Chapin

I had a particularly busy temple week. Meetings every night for one thing or another with the goings on of our temple. Now I'm not complaining. I knew what I was getting myself into when this all started. In fact, to the contrary, despite the time commitment of a week like this, I'm rather excited because of this activity. Yes, it is a lot a meetings and yes, it can be exhausting. But whether it is a board meeting, or a committee meeting to discuss our programming, or planning for our temple's future, there is a satisfaction in knowing that I, along with so many other volunteers, are part of a one hundred and eighty year history, and that we are, and have always been, a forward thinking congregation, one that takes care of today and is always looking toward tomorrow.

The late great singer songwriter Harry Chapin once gave an interview where he talked about his grandfather who told him, ""Harry, there's two kinds of tired. There's good tired and there's bad tired." He said, "Ironically enough, bad tired can be a day that you won. But you won other people's battles; you lived other people's days, other people's agendas, other people's dreams. And when it's all over, there was very little you in there. And when you hit the hay at night, somehow you toss and turn; you don't settle easy."

His grandfather continued: "Good tired, ironically enough, can be a day that you lost, but you don't even have to tell yourself because you knew you fought your battles, you chased your dreams, you lived your days and when you hit the hay at night, you settle easy, you sleep the sleep of the just and you say 'take me away'"

Busy as this week was, there was a lot of US in it. We discussed today and our future, we worked on OUR agenda, and worked toward chasing our temple's long term dreams. And after this week, I can say, I am good tired! On this Shabbat, may you all feel good tired too!

Shabbat Shalom

Expectations

With our beloved Cincinnati Reds having a historic season (2022) – unfortunately, historic for all the wrong reasons – I started thinking about the nature of baseball and what qualifies for success.

I know I am not the first person to say this, and so I'll quote a baseball loving rabbi, about whom I read, that said, "Errors are part of the game, failure is common, and one in three is greatness". Baseball is one of the few contexts in which failure is built into the game and a 300 lifetime batting average is considered great, and yet that person makes an out seven out of every ten at bats.

We say on Yom Kippur, "who among us has not sinned", or in more simpler terms, those used in our children's high holiday book of old, "who among us has not missed the mark". We all miss the mark on occasion, hopefully not 7 out of 10 times, but we still certainly do.

Why is it that we cannot accept such standards as baseball in our everyday lives. Sometimes our expectations are so high for others in our lives that they cannot possibly live up to those expectations. And why is that we can't accept that we can still be a good person despite a failure, or an error in our own life. We hold ourselves to these same high expectations, which on one hand is good – it sets goals for us and allows us to strive to be better people each day, but it also prevents us from letting ourselves off the hook every once in a while.

We can all surely do better. But on the occasion where someone in your life may miss the mark, or perhaps you miss the mark, remember the baseball analogy. And remember: none of us can bat one thousand.

On this Shabbat, let us remember to show patience and understanding when someone misses the mark, and hope that others will show the same towards us when we too fall short.

Shabbat Shalom

Jewish Commonality

Tomorrow morning, I'll be attending an aufruf ceremony at our neighbor temple. The bride, who grew up in Boston, is the daughter of someone I know from growing up here in Cincinnati. The bride's grandfather was once a Rabbi here in Cincinnati. And the groom is the son of some local friends. How they met is typical of Jewish geography - parents involved, connections made, etc. Didn't want to meet at first, and then somehow connected, and the rest as they say…

I have talked about my own Jewish connections before - they stretch far and wide. From camp, from NFTY, from college. And my kids connections also stretch far and wide. For my kids, it was camp, NFTY, college and also Israel trips that made their connections. As they graduate and move on with their lives, these connections will ensure that they know people in almost any major city across the United States. I have often told my own kids that regardless of how they express their Judaism in their lives, there is always some comfort in meeting other Jews, simply because of the commonality that is felt almost immediately. Somehow, there will be something in common. They will know someone who knows someone. From someplace or another, be it NFTY, camp, college or an Israel trip. There is an ease and comfort upon meeting someone Jewish because you know there will be this commonality. And so was the story with the couple being celebrated tomorrow.

Having the temple, our temple, as a place for our kids to begin these connections is such an important starting point. Then layer in the places of informal Jewish education such as NFTY and camp, and their ability to find common ground with seeming strangers becomes almost second nature. My kids didn't believe me at first, but they have often reported to me that I was right.

As a parent, we cannot choose the path for our kids, but we can hopefully set them up for success. And one part of that is starting them on the path to these Jewish connections.

On this Shabbat, let us teach our children to make these Jewish connections, ones that will serve them throughout their lives, and who knows, maybe even lead them to the chuppah.

Shabbat Shalom

The Beatles

For our Fab Four Beatles Shabbat:

MAYBE I'M AMAZED at our attendance here tonight. I've searched all ACROSS THE UNIVERSE, and am yet to find anything like the THINGS WE SAID TODAY here tonight. I'VE GOT A FEELING, that WITH A LITTLE HELP FROM MY FRIENDS, we created a beautiful space HERE THERE AND EVERYWHERE tonight and I hope that the Sabbath spirit has moved WITHIN YOU WITHOUT YOU. You know that Sabbath bride – SHE LOVES YOU.

The Sabbath reveals our truest selves, so that we can ACT NATURALLY, and COME TOGETHER as a community to share the ideal that ALL YOU NEED IS LOVE, and truly allow THE INNER LIGHT to shine.

Don't ASK ME WHY, but perhaps you can TELL ME WHY there's SOMETHING, something special about this night. Or perhaps, that question can go unanswered, and we'll LET IT BE. I SHOULD HAVE KNOWN BETTER than to bring that up.

All I know is that tonight, I FEEL FINE. And so, here at THE END of my thoughts, on this Shabbat, FROM ME TO YOU, I wish you all GOLDEN SLUMBERS tonight and a GOOD DAY SUNSHINE tomorrow, with the melody of HERE COMES THE SUN giving you warmth and peace. And let us say, ALL TOGETHER NOW: Shabbat Shalom

Music in Me

I'm going to date myself, but one of my favorite songs growing up was a song called I've Got the Music in Me – by Kiki Dee – 1974, if you're scoring at home. Tonight, that's how I feel – I've got the music in me. We are so grateful to have our musician in residence here tonight and for the entire weekend. Having grown up and worked as a songleader at our regional summer camp, Goldman Union Camp, Jewish music has been an integral part of my life. There is a feeling I get when I hear the guitar playing Jewish music that takes me back to a time and a place. I can only hope you appreciate it as much as I do.

On this Shabbat, may we be able to say, "I've Got the Music in Me!", to allow music to seep into your soul, and to give you the warmth that comes from memory.

Shabbat Shalom

Laughter

I don't usually make humorous comments in my typical Friday greetings. But I am finding more and more, that a little laughter goes a long way. And I am seeking places where even the smallest laugh, which also inevitably brings a smile, appear during my day.

So in an effort to elicit some laughs, here goes:

From the Henny Youngman collection:
A car hit a Jewish man. The paramedic says, "Are you

comfortable?" The man says, "I make a good living."

And from a simple google search about the best Jewish jokes – you judge for yourself:

A little Jewish boy was telling his mother about how he had won a part in a play that was being done at school. His mother asked, "What is the part you will play?" And the child responded, "I shall play the Jewish husband," to which the mother replied, "Well, you go right back to that teacher and tell her that you want a SPEAKING part!"

From the Mayo clinic's site I learned that a good laugh has short term and long term health benefits. In the short term, it activates and relieves your stress response, and soothes tension. And in the long term, laughter can improve your immune system, relieve pain, and the obvious one, improve your mood.

We've all been dealing with some fairly heavy things these past weeks, and one five minute stretch of watching the evening news is enough to frighten us most nights. So let's take a little respite from the news cycle, and seek out a little laughter. What a great resolution to find a way to laugh and smile each day. We all deserve some stress relief, an immune system boost and an improvement to our moods.

On this Shabbat, and every day, may we find a way to giggle like a little baby and bring more laughter and smiles into our lives and the lives of our friends and family.

Shabbat Shalom

Christmas on Shabbat

Christmas on Shabbat? Or is it Shabbat on Christmas? I wondered – how often does this happen? And I found out that it is part of a cycle on our calendar that happens every six or eleven years. The last time it happened was 2010 and the next time is 2027. However, due to the quirks that leap year puts into our calendar, there is an extra time here and there. So it happens more often than you might think.

While we often do community service work on Christmas, to help others so that they may have time off to be with their families, or to help those in need, the question arises: what are we supposed to do when Christmas falls on Shabbat. Shabbat is our day of rest, and while spending time with family on Shabbat is something we strive for, the idea of working on Shabbat, even if it is community service, is in conflict with what our Sabbath is meant to be.

In thinking about this, I remembered something said to me many years ago. This was part of a lesson being taught at Goldman Union Camp, the summer camp where I spent many years as a teenager. The lesson suggested that in today's modern world, it is so much harder to simply rest and do nothing on shabbat. Perhaps a more modern and Reform Jewish perspective on Shabbat was to the make the day different – to make it stand out from the rest of the days of the week - to do things on Shabbat such that while they may not be actual rest, they revive you in a spiritual way and are things only reserved for this day of the week, so that this day still stands out from the rest. This is a great way for us to look at Shabbat on Christmas. And what better way to have a Shabbat on Christmas than to work tomorrow at a soup kitchen, and then join with family.

Just as we make something of our fast on Yom Kippur by providing food to those in need, perhaps we can also make something of our Shabbat on Christmas, setting aside this day to make it different than any other and in doing so, make a difference.

Shabbat Shalom

Extra Rewards

I spent the last week of the year in Sedona, Arizona. That might sound like a luxurious winter vacation, but alas, it was not. Instead of sand and beaches, we had rain and snow and thirty degree weather with cloudy skies almost the entire week. Some of our plans were cancelled due to the weather.

This was a family vacation – including my parents, my brothers and all of our wives and kids. From that aspect it was as wonderful as always. We don't get to spend that much time together given that I have a brother on the west coast. So having a full week of quality time together was the saving grace.

Sedona is famous for its red rocks and mountains. But amidst the dreary sky, those red rocks are not always evident. However, one of the amazing things about those dreary skies, is that every so often, there is a slight break in the clouds and a tiny bit of sunlight comes through. This phenomenon is like nothing we ever see in our part of the world. And when this happens, there is a bit of magic that occurs.

This photo is not edited or photoshopped. We were driving down the road when a small break in the clouds allowed sun to shine on just this part of the mountainside. We immediately pulled over and took a photo. And we were not the only people doing so – there were a number of other cars that did just the same. And within ten seconds of getting back in the car, the break in the clouds closed and the sun was gone.

We spent the whole week looking for those breaks in the clouds, for that little bit of magic and every so often we were rewarded with beautiful and majestic scenery and that little bit of warmth. We had warmth within the family, but it was so nice to have that complemented by warmth from mother nature.

As we start a new year, may we all continue to find those extra rewards that appear to us, if only we would look for them.

Shabbat Shalom

Service to Others

In my role as President, I'm often tasked with asking congregants to volunteer for certain things, such as positions on committees, working on various programs, or participating in our many volunteer activities. This week was no exception. It never ceases to amaze me the response I receive during these conversations. We are so incredibly lucky to have congregants who care so deeply about our temple and are so willing to give of their time and energy. One comment during a conversation this week is worth repeating here: this congregant made it clear that despite a very busy schedule with work and kids, and other volunteering that she does, she was still willing to help because, in her words, our temple had done so much for her family since they joined many years ago.

We serve our congregants and in turn, they want to serve us and others. Could there be higher praise for any temple?

And so I ask, if you are not already volunteering at the Temple, to please consider helping too. If you truly appreciate what our temple has meant to you and your family, your volunteering can help so many people and inspire other congregants to do the same. This is not a request for money! This is a request for action, and I'm sure you can find a way to contribute.

On this Shabbat, let us consider the ways in which our temple has enriched our lives, so that we may in turn, enrich the lives of others.

Shabbat Shalom

Love's in Need of Love Today

Admittedly, this one is a bit sappy, but I figure a little sap is okay around the holidays.

Spotify is just great. I can get anything anytime with very few exceptions. And every so often I try to create some new playlists for myself. This past week, it was a Stevie Wonder playlist and I came across a song I hadn't heard in years. Written in 1976 is the song "Love's in need of love today. " Here are the lyrics that caught my ear:

Love's in need of love today
Don't delay

Send yours in right away
Hate's goin' round
Breaking many hearts
Stop it please, before it's gone too far

These words were written in the 70's, and yet could have been written today as a reflection of our own time. Hate IS going round, perhaps at an even more alarming rate than when this song was written.

Hate is learned, and we repeatedly see it taught at an early age, completing a cycle the parents had as children. Antisemitism, Racism, Islamophobia – all taught to children by parents. But hate can also be unlearned. And sappy as it may sound, the way to unlearn hate is to do so with love.

Just last night on the evening news was a story of a Black family moving to Lubbock Texas, in a school district where their son is subject to racism on a daily basis. The other students certainly were not born hating – it was learned, and yet the boy is showing dignity and grace in trying to make the other students understand that despite skin color, there is more that makes them alike than different. We need to unlearn hate by re-learning how to love. And by teaching our children the value of love.

On this Shabbat, when love is indeed in need of love, please don't delay, send yours in right away, before it's gone too far. And be a light to others to do the same.

Shabbat Shalom

Shabbat

I have mentioned before that, everyday, I read a book called Life's Daily Blessings, by Rabbi Kerry Olitzky – with a quote or statement from some Jewish text and then a brief commentary for each day of the year.

In the past few days I read this quote from the Babylonian Talmud:

A person should always set a table AFTER Shabbat even if one is quite full and satisfied.

The commentary for this quote suggests that having a feast on

Saturday night is a way to express gratitude for Shabbat and the desire to keep Shabbat going as long as possible, even if there has been a true day of rest that satisfies the soul.

I spent many summers at Goldman Union Camp, where Shabbat is the focus of each week. It is celebrated with a special meal, lots of singing and dancing, and a total break from the regular weekly schedule of camp. At camp, you are immersed in a true day of rest, a true Shabbat experience.

However, the daily demands of our lives make such a true respite difficult. And yet we try. We are here, starting Shabbat with our own T'fillah – Sabbath service. And once we are done here, starts the challenge to make the remaining time until tomorrow night a full and satisfying Shabbat, one that renews and energizes you for the next week ahead.

On this Shabbat, I hope that you find time to enjoy a respite from the week, and to rest and recharge, so that you are quite full and satisfied.

Shabbat Shalom

Country Music

Okay, I admit it. I love country music. Just listen to some of these lyrics:

From Jordan Davis and Luke Bryan:
Find the one you can't live without
Get a ring, let your knee hit the ground
Do what you love but call it work
And throw a little money in the plate at church
Send your prayers up and your roots down deep
And add a few limbs to your family tree
And watch their pencil marks

And the grass in the yard all grow up

From Travis Tritt:
I was sittin' at a table
In a little club downtown
Playin' songs on the jukebox
And pourin' whiskey down
When I heard a sweet voice sayin'
"Would you like some company?"
And I had to tell her
This is just between
an old memory and me

From Kenny Chesney:
Cause the one thing stronger than the whiskey
Was the sight of her holdin' my baby girl

The way she adored that string of pearls
I gave her the day that our youngest boy, Earl
Married his high school love'
Yeah, man, that's the good stuff

From Zac Brown:
Well its funny how it's the little things in life that mean the most
Not where you live or what you drive or the price tag on your clothes
There's no dollar sign on a peace of mind this I've come to know
So if you agree have a drink with me
Raise your glasses for a toast
To a little bit of chicken fried

And from Darius Rucker:
The only B.S. I need is beers and sunshine

The rhyme schemes, the imagery, the simple stories, the acoustic guitars – that all works for me. Of course, there are some overarching themes in country music – beer or whiskey, God, love of country, trucks, and anything having to do with affairs of the heart - new love, old love, heartache or heartbreak. Other than "trucks", I'd argue that these themes are universal for us as Americans.

Over the past few years, we've been tested, especially with our love of country. We may be angry, but we need to be reminded of these themes that make us more alike than different. Maybe that's the power of this music and why I like it so much.

You may mock me for my love of country music, but whether its country, rock, folk, jazz, hip hop, showtunes, or even Jewish music, there is a power in those melodies. Music brings an emotional response, sometimes even tears, and that is just what we need to remind of us of our basic decency and our humanity. In music, and do I dare say, in country music, we actually find common ground.

So give these country songs a chance. You may find that you love them, or perhaps just come to appreciate them more. They tug at your heart strings and reach a place deep down inside.

On this Shabbat, I hope you'll listen to some country music and allow yourselves to get lost in the stories, the emotions, the beauty of the acoustic guitar, sounds we can all relate to and that have the power to bring us together.

Shabbat Shalom

Making a Difference

As of last Saturday, our congregation has decided to sponsor an Afghan refugee family. They are a family of six and it is now incumbent upon us to literally take care of their every need so that they can get established here in Cincinnati. We have an amazing committee of volunteers who have the incredible responsibility of helping them to get settled. This involves finding housing, finding transportation, finding jobs, getting kids enrolled in school, getting driver's licenses and other necessary documentation, buying groceries, learning how American grocery stores even work, getting bank accounts set up, and learning the American banking system. And this is nowhere near an exhaustive list. There is so much more. Our committee meets once a week to review the needs and make a plan for how to address those needs each coming week. It really is quite remarkable.

The 20th century theologian Abraham Joshua Heschel wrote about the Hebrew prophets and saw the teachings of the prophets as a call to social action in the United States. He worked tirelessly for civil rights and I believe there is a lot we can learn from his writings. One quote from Heschel that I always find so interesting is this: *"When I was young, I admired clever people. Now that I am old, I admire kind people."*

With age comes the wisdom to know that it is kindness and love that make the difference in our lives, and the difference we can make in others' lives. And we are making a difference in the lives of our Afghan family.

On this Shabbat, and every day, may we hear the call to make a difference and offer kindness to others.

Shabbat Shalom

Connection to Action

When we adopted a family seeking asylum from Afghanistan, we asked for help with items needed by this family. There was a link to the various items set up on Amazon. Within a day of the email going out, everything on the Amazon wish list was purchased. And I imagine it was really without thought at all, more of a reflex, recognizing a family in need and immediately acting. Selfless acts to say the least.

Clearly, this connected with people.

If only we could EACH find something we connect with that

strongly. How much of a better place we could make the world. Some cause or some need that we could address simply because we felt called to work on it. We could all actively participate in Tikkun Olam, the process of repairing the world.

From the oral traditions known as the Mishnah, specifically Pirke Avot, we are taught that, "we need not complete the work, but neither are we free to desist from it." And also from Pirke Avot, we are taught that, "If I am not for myself, who will be for me, if I am only for myself, what am I, and if not now, when."

So perhaps we need to ask ourselves, is it time not just to be for yourself, but also to be for others, and then recognize that the time is now. The time for action is always now. The question is, what is it that connects with you and spurs you to that action. Our tradition calls you toward these tasks, even if you are not the one to complete it.

On this Shabbat, may you search deeply to find a cause with which you connect, to be for yourself and others and to act now.

Shabbat Shalom

Not Alone

Prior to becoming President, I was invited to attend the Scheidt Seminar, which is hosted by the URJ and intended for those about to become a congregational President. I say "attended" but it was in a pandemic world, and attending meant being on a lot of zoom meetings for a four day weekend.

As a follow up from that seminar, we were asked to participate in a Presidents Network, in which we were assigned to groups of six fellow "soon to be" Presidents, all from congregations of similar size.

My group consists of Temple Presidents from congregations in Atlanta, Houston, Washington D.C., Baltimore and Boston and we have all now begun our terms as President. We were asked to meet once a month and to try and discuss a new topic each month. However, most of this year, our agendas have been consumed by pandemic discussions and what's going on in each of our congregations. My latest meeting was just last night and I wanted to share some of that discussion.

All our congregations continue to deal with our pandemic challenges, such as the wearing of masks, finding new ways to use technology for services and adult education, and learning about what post pandemic life will look like. And yet, we also all have experienced great commitment from our congregants - in program participation and financial contributions during this time, in spite of the pandemic. The generosity of our congregants in this most uncertain time is a consistent theme in our discussion, which is amazing. That has been one of the most encouraging messages emanating from these meetings.

I take comfort in knowing that these challenges are not unique to our temple – it gives me hope that across the country there are dedicated individuals working in their congregations as we are in ours with the goal towards making our congregations stronger. We are emerging stronger AND smarter and I look forward with anticipation at what is to come.

Shabbat Shalom

Summer Camp

With all that has been going on these past few weeks in our news cycle, I thought tonight I would focus on something a bit lighter.

As is typical for me this time of year, my thoughts turn toward summer camp, and in particular Goldman Union Camp – our regional reform Jewish camp, outside of Indianapolis. On Facebook, I am "friends" with camp so I see daily postings with photos of what is going on so far during the first session for this summer. Those updates telling me what was served for breakfast, lunch and dinner along with the activities for the day always bring a smile to my face.

One of my funniest memories dates to when I was on staff. Ironically, on whatever was the hottest day of the session, the lunch served was hot tomato soup and grilled cheese. The camp director, Rabbi Ron Klotz would go around saying "nothing like hot soup on a hot day" as if he was trying to provide us some divine guidance to explain to all the camp kids why on earth hot soup would be served on the hottest day, and to make us believe that hot soup really was good for us on a hot day. What else could he do, but make the most of the situation. I still think about this whenever I see anyone eat tomato soup and grilled cheese.

And how about these other lessons learned from Jewish summer camp outlined in a Huffington Post article written a number of years ago:

-You can legitimately fall in love in less than a week
-Patience is a skill. It was a struggle to have to wait to eat until everyone said a blessing over the food at every single meal
-Anything, including cleaning bathrooms, washing dishes and picking up trash -- can be fun if you are doing it with friends to help keep

a place that you love running smoothly.

-How to keep in touch with faraway friends over the course of the year. Learning that childhood friendships can span across the country, and can be maintained for longer than you'd ever imagine.

Goldman Union Camp is all of that and more to me. I experienced all of the above and watched so many of my friends do so as well. Friends, I might add that I still keep in touch with even though my last official summer at camp was 1989. Friends living not just in our camp area but in Boston, L.A., New York, Chicago,

Dallas, Toronto, Detroit, San Francisco, and more.

For those of you that went to Jewish summer camp, or any summer camp, I hope you maintain those fond memories too. And for those that did not, think about sending your kids and asking the grandparents to help pay for it. There is no better gift to help shape the Jewish identity of your child.

On this Shabbat, may we reminisce about summers gone by, allowing those memories to continue bringing us joy all these years later.

Shabbat Shalom

Thankful at Temple

In the spirit of the approaching Thanksgiving Holiday, I thought I would reflect tonight on what I am thankful for and grateful for about our temple.

I'm thankful to be a part of a community that truly cares about the well-being of its members.

I'm thankful to be part of an incredibly diverse congregation - diverse in age, diverse in zip codes across our greater Cincinnati area, diverse in viewpoints, diverse in the careers of its members, diverse in the needs and wants of its members.

I'm thankful to have an amazing, talented and dedicated Board of Trustees and Executive Board with whom I can collaborate and with whom we can put our best feet forward to keep our congregation moving forward as well.

I'm thankful for our incredible Rabbinic leadership and the guidance and teaching they provide for us every day of the year. They are here in times of joy, times of sadness, and everywhere in between.

I'm thankful for our incredible staff – most of who you do not even see.

But they are here working diligently to support all we do at Temple.

I'm thankful for being part of a truly active congregation – social action, educational, and social programs abound, some for our cohorts within the congregation, and others for the entire congregation. Hardly a day goes by without some type of programming being offered.

And I'm thankful for the fact that as President, I have brought Shabbat more firmly into focus in my life, simply by being here each week.

As Thanksgiving approaches, may you find as many things to be thankful about, not just at our temple, but with your families and friends as well.

Shabbat Shalom

Thankful Part 2

For this Thanksgiving week, here are things I'm thankful for this year:

The love of my wife and family
Really talented and caring doctors and nurses
Medical science
A great meal
A perfect chocolate malt
My sons making me so proud to be their father
The guitar
The music of the Beatles, Billy Joel, James Taylor, Harry Chapin, Bruce Springsteen, Broadway musicals, and some country artists too numerous to mention

The sound of Kol Nidrei played on the cello and the way it makes me feel when I hear it
Our incredible temple community – c'mon now, you didn't think I'd leave out the temple, did you?

But I am thankful for temple perhaps in a different way than you might think. As a temple community we provide so much to our congregants – learning opportunities from pre-school to our oldest congregants, community action opportunities, civic engagement, opportunities to connect with each other in social settings, not to mention opportunities for worship and spiritual fulfillment. I certainly hope those are reasons you are thankful for our temple.

For me, though, there is something else. Serving as president affords me an opportunity to give back to a temple that has been a part of my entire life, not just with my dues, but with time and energy. I know that many in our congregation can't always give what they may want through dues, but there is always a way to give of your time and energy that can certainly make a difference.

And I am also thankful for our executive board, our board of trustees, and our temple staff that support me and help us to realize the vision of our congregation.

On this Shabbat of Thanksgiving, let us consider what we are thankful for, and ways we can give back that will allow others to be thankful.

Shabbat Shalom

Softball

If you receive the American Israelite newspaper, then you saw last week's cover story about the Jewish Center Men's Fastpitch Softball League. It's been around since 1945, and I've been fortunate to be a part of it for many of the last twenty five years. It's serious stuff – each player is drafted, it is fast pitch, we have umpires, stealing and bunting. And as you can imagine – there are some guys who take it way too seriously, all the more fun to watch for an average player like me.

But the league takes all who apply, regardless of talent level. And the best part of our league is the family rule. If you have a brother, son, or grandson, you can be guaranteed to play on the same team as your family member. And yes, brothers play together, fathers and sons play together, and even grandfathers and grandsons have played together.

There are certain families that can mark their participation in the league all the way back to the start. That is really special to watch.

Even better is the fact that most of the guys go out for some food and a beer each week after the game to regale in old stories and new ones, creating new friendships and cementing old ones.

In an era of so much busy-ness, the softball league is a place where Jewish men connect. We are so fortunate to have our own such place here with our Brotherhood – the men of our congregation who meet to socialize and do amazing work for our temple community and the community at large. We are grateful to have them!

On this Shabbat, let us remember that what is common among us is so much stronger than what is different. And let us continue to find ways to seek out those avenues where we can cultivate and cement friendships.

Shabbat Shalom

Brisket

This past week, I've been thinking a lot about one topic, and that topic is Brisket. Of course, my mom served brisket at our seder last Friday. My brother had a second seder where he invited many of his daughters' non Jewish friends to allow them to experience Passover. What did they serve – brisket. And I was offered some of the leftovers to both of these seders. Then on Monday night, we had an executive board meeting, and what was the one of the topics of discussion as we were all joining our meeting - you guessed it – brisket.

Now naturally, my mom's recipe for brisket is the best. But then, I'm sure you'd say the same, except perhaps instead of your mom, it's your grandmother, or even great grandmother.

Here's a little history lesson on brisket – it has been eaten by Jews going back to the 1700's. It was considered a lesser cut of beef, and thus much more affordable, especially to those living in the shtetl. But what we Jews found out was that if you cooked it low and slow, it became very tender and as we all know, delicious. Now every deli and bbq diner in America better have brisket or else be considered second rate at best. The Jews are to thank for that.

What is it about brisket that makes us so happy and that caused me to think about it so much this week? Like most Jewish holidays, Passover starts with family, as we all gather for seder. And so for me, I relate brisket to family. The only time I ever eat a nice brisket dinner is when my whole family is together, be it Rosh Hashanah, Passover or some other special family occasion. It's our "go to" family meal. All the way back to my childhood, brisket represents my family being together for one reason or another. Pretty amazing that this lesser cut of beef could be so powerful in my mind.

So I'll ask – what does brisket mean to you? What memories does it conjure in your mind? I only hope they are as wonderfully nostalgic as mine.

On this Shabbat, let us meditate on the meaning of brisket, and be thankful for the gathering of family together.

Shabbat Shalom

Laughter Part 2

I've wondered, why don't we laugh more while we're here at temple? Now there is nothing inherently funny about services, but still I wondered. We come here on Shabbat for a break from the week, to relax, unwind, pray, and what's wrong with a little humor along the way.

I read this: "In Judaism, religion and humor are not antithetical. A rabbi is even required to have a sense of humor, since the Talmud says that before a session of Torah study, a good teacher tells a joke to expand his pupils' minds." I'll put our rabbis to this task for their next Talmud class.

So to bring humor here tonight, I thought I'd experiment with AI, artificial intelligence. I went to an AI website that my son works for to see if it could produce some Jewish humor. I was able to input requests about Jewish humor while attending services, or Jewish humor about a rabbi and sermons. The results were disastrous. None were funny, so much so that I won't repeat any of the output here, lest you all groan.

A computer can't bring humor to our Temple. There is clearly a nuance to Jewish humor that a machine can't yet grasp. I'd be better off simply referencing a shared experience, like Mel Brooks holding three tablets of fifteen commandments, dropping one tablet, and then boldly pronouncing them the Ten Commandments, or something as simple as when Tevye, in Fiddler on the Roof says, "I know, I know, we are your chosen people, but once in a while, can't you choose someone else?" This is humor we share that enhances our experience, even here at temple.

So here's an experiment for us all to try tonight: Smile big when you leave the chapel tonight, while you're wishing each other Shabbat

Shalom, and even throw in a joke to whoever you may be speaking to. And next week, and each week when you arrive, try to do the same as you greet each other in the lobby for a nosh before temple. Perhaps it will make you feel better, even if just for a minute. In this way, we'll add some humor to temple, expand our minds, and fulfill our responsibility to lift each other up as part of a community.

On this Shabbat, let us look for the humor in life, even at temple, and find more ways to smile and laugh.

Shabbat Shalom

Passover – Rabbi Nachman

Many of you may have heard of the Baal Shem Tov, the founder of the Chasidic movement who lived in the early 1700's. But perhaps you have not heard of his equally quotable great grandson, Rabbi Nachman of Breslov, of the late 1700's. Rabbi Nachman said this about Passover - "The Exodus from Egypt occurs in every human being, in every era, in every year, and in every day."

According to Rabbi Nachman, it is as if we, ourselves, were at Mt. Sinai. As a result, each of us has in our DNA the feeling, the experience of having been there. That is why we re-tell the story every year at our seders. We are compelled to do so, as if re-living our own personal past. And by re-telling, we remind ourselves of the importance of helping others whose plight is like our own.

As Reform Jews, our history informs us. We are to learn from it and apply that learning to our modern world. Today, we watch so many others around the world who continue to endure their own Exodus. What happened in Egypt HAS happened in every era, in every year, and almost every day. Maybe not to us, but to others around the world.

I encourage you to find a way to get involved. Do your part. You heard our Rabbi say just a few weeks ago, we may not be able to change the world, but we can change one person's world, or one family's world. Our retelling of the Exodus story implores us to remember our suffering so that we might help others.

On this Shabbat, and next week, as we prepare for Passover, let us not forget that we were slaves in Egypt, let that remembrance cause us to work with others toward a goal of peace and equality so that, rather than an Exodus in every era, we can say there is peace for every human, in every era, every year, and every day.

Shabbat Shalom

Purim Lessons

We are on the cusp of Purim, so I thought I'd try to learn more about our Purim customs.

Hamantaschen is of course our most delicious custom. And there is also the custom of wearing costumes and finding joy and happiness on the holiday. The Talmud goes so far as to give this advice for drinking on Purim "A person has to drink on Purim until he cannot distinguish between 'cursed is Haman' and 'blessed is Mordechai." Use this Talmudic advice with caution, especially if driving. Safety of a person always takes precedence over any other commandment.

Another custom is the giving of Mishloach Manot – literally, "sending of portions", which are gifts of food to friends and also to families in need. In this way, we add meaning to the holiday outside of the silliness and joy of the day.

And then we are also commanded to listen to the Purim Story. I find it very interesting that we are commanded to listen to and re-tell the story each year, similar to how we are commanded to re-tell the story of the exodus each year on Passover.

According to the Talmud, "the study of Torah is interrupted for the reading of the Megillah." And Maimonides taught that, "the reading of the Megillah certainly supersedes all other mitzvot."

What is it about us as Jews when it comes to reading and re-telling our history. As Reform Jews, we are certainly not stuck in the past, and yet perhaps the essence of Reform Judaism is our tradition of continuing to be the people of the book, and our willingness to use that knowledge to live in the modern world. We've heard our own rabbis preach for years that the reason we read the Torah portion each week is not because the portion changes from year to year, but it's because WE change, and each year we have something new to bring to the portion. And so it is with Purim. Each year we listen to the story, make noise with our groggers when we hear that one certain name, but also hopefully glean something new that we may not have considered in years past. The Purim story of antisemitism certainly rings loudly as a continuing lesson today.

As Purim approaches, let us follow the commandment to be happy because it's Adar, to increase joy, to be silly, but also follow the commandment to re-tell the story, and in doing so, re-listen to its messages, to try to glean some new meaning for our world today.

Shabbat Shalom

Be Happy

Be Happy, It's Adar – yes that is our mantra for this current Jewish month. So without further ado, here are some sayings about being happy:

Happiness is when what you think, what you say and what you do are in harmony. Mahatma Gandhi

It is only possible to live happily ever after on a daily basis. Margaret Bonanno

Don't worry, be happy. Bobby McFerrin

Happiness depends upon ourselves.
Aristotle

If you want happiness for an hour—take a nap. If you want happiness for a day—go fishing. If you want happiness for a year—inherit a fortune. If you want happiness for a lifetime—help someone else.
Chinese Proverb

Happiness is not in the mere possession of money; it lies in the joy of achievement, in the thrill of creative effort. Franklin Roosevelt

Better an ounce of happiness than a pound of gold. Jewish Proverb

Most people are about as happy as they make up their minds to be. Abraham Lincoln

Success is getting what you want. Happiness is wanting what you get. Dale Carnegie

Who is wealthy? Those who are happy with their lot. Pirke Avot

Let no one ever come to you without leaving better and happier. Mother Teresa

Those who are not looking for happiness are the most likely to find it, because those who are searching forget that the surest way to be happy is to seek happiness for others. Martin Luther King Jr.

Whoever is happy will make others happy too. Anne Frank

On this Shabbat, and for this month of Adar, let us focus on not only our happiness, but making those around us happy as well.

Shabbat Shalom

Off to College

What a special night for us as we recognize our high school seniors, who have been committed and dedicated to our temple their entire lives in one way or another. Religious School, youth group, bar/bat mitzvah, confirmation, madrichim and perhaps Jewish summer camp – it is pretty incredible how much of their lives has been tied to our temple. Whether they realized it or not, this was and is a second home. And now, off you go into the world, without the temple as one of your anchors. How strange and wonderful and exciting it is to go into the unknown and find your way.

We are always looking for answers, and often we are rewarded with the information we seek. But those answers are not always forthcoming, and that is okay.

Albert Einstein said this:
The most beautiful thing we can experience is the mysterious. It is the source of all true art and science. He to whom the emotion is a stranger, who can no longer pause to wonder and stand wrapped in awe, is as good as dead – his eyes are closed.

So to our seniors we say: go out into the world, experience new things, stand in wonder and awe at our world. And let it be okay that you can't figure it all out. There is beauty in the mysterious. Eventually you'll find out what you need, but leave some of the mystery. We wish our seniors, nothing more than the beauty of experiencing the mysteries of our world and finding their way in it, hoping that what they've learned along the way, including what they've learned at our temple, will serve them well in their discovery.

And this is a great lesson for all of us, reveling in the fact that we can't know it all. Enjoying that we still have some mysteriousness in our world and knowing that there are experiences out there for us to explore. We spend so much time tied to facts and news. We need to allow ourselves time to wonder.

On this Shabbat, may we all pause, take time out from our weekly routines, and take a moment to gaze at the stars like Einstein did, to find some beauty in the mysterious.

Shabbat Shalom

One Year Difference

What a difference one year can make. We've seen what can happen in the life of others in just one year if we commit ourselves to helping in the community.

In the life of our planet, which is four and half billion years old, one single year is statistically insignificant, and yet the damage we are doing each single year is becoming irreparable.

Consider this from the New York Times this week – an article about the report from the Intergovernmental Panel on Climate Change, a panel of experts convened by the United Nations. The report says that global average temperatures are estimated to rise 1.5 degrees Celsius above preindustrial levels sometime around "the first half of the 2030s," as humans continue to burn coal, oil and natural gas.

That number holds a special significance because beyond that point, scientists say, the impacts of catastrophic heat waves, flooding, drought, crop failures and species extinction become significantly harder for humanity to handle. And the solution would require industrialized nations to join together immediately to slash greenhouse gases roughly in half by 2030 and then stop adding carbon dioxide to the atmosphere altogether by the early 2050's. If those two steps were taken, the world would still only have about a 50 percent chance of limiting warming to 1.5 degrees Celsius. And further delays of even a few years would most likely make that goal unattainable, guaranteeing a hotter, more perilous future.

Think of the things we can't agree on in our country – there are too many to count. But this should not be one of them. These are facts, agreed upon by an entire scientific community. And this is about our children and our grandchildren.

I have used this quote before, but it is so appropriate here: From Pirke Avot: Lo alecha hamlacha ligmor; v'lo atah ben chorin l'hibatel mimena. It is not your duty to finish the work, but neither are you free to desist from it.

The time to act is now. Give yourself a year and see what changes you can make. Those changes could involve your own personal behaviors with regard to climate change, or your activism in helping the community and world at large. That is my challenge for you here tonight.

On this Shabbat, let us consider where we want to be three hundred and sixty five days from now and see what a difference a year can make.

Shabbat Shalom

Hometown Sports

One of the big stories in Cincinnati this week was the dismantling of the Reds by team ownership. Now the Reds really only have a handful of good players, or should I say – HAD a handful of good players. One by one, they were traded away in a fire sale this week.

What is it about our hometown sports teams that generate so much emotion in us. We know it's just a game. And yet, when they don't do well, we feel as though that is somehow a reflection on us and our city. We are so caught up in what is going on and we take our sports teams' successes and failures so seriously and so personally.

One sportscaster I love to listen to likes to remind his audience that the word fan comes from fanatic. And he recommends that in order to feel less disappointed by our sports teams, we should perhaps ease up on being a fanatic. He says – Like your sports team, but Love your family. So I have fallen out of love with my hometown teams – that might sound harsh, especially for a kid that grew up in Cincinnati in the 70's with the Big Red Machine and attended the freezer bowl victory of the Bengals over the Chargers. But I'll tell you - I'm better for it. I really like my teams, and I support them, but now they won't rip my heart out when I see something like what I watched this week with the Reds. And I can reserve my fanaticism for my family. I love my family.

On this Shabbat, and every day forward, let us be fans "in like" of our sports teams and fanatics "in love" with our families.

Shabbat Shalom

Volunteering

As my term nears its conclusion in a few weeks, I have been thinking back on the past two years, and I found myself looking at what volunteering has meant to me. Because, whether you knew it or not, I was not paid for this gig. I was jokingly promised a salary of one penny, but to date, have not been paid.

There is much written about volunteering. One article listed the benefits of volunteering that fit perfectly with my experience and I'll share some of that with you here.

First, volunteering connects you to others. Having grown up at our temple, I thought I knew so many of our congregants. But serving as President put me in a position to connect with so many more of our congregants. It is that type of connection that we can all use to help strengthen our ties to our temple. The more we are connected, the more valuable this place can become. When we feel those connections, we form stronger and more meaningful relationships.

Second, volunteering is good for your mind and body. I cannot count how many times I was caught up in my own world, worried, anxious, and busy. But when I shifted to temple business, my attitude and emotions changed – there is power in knowing you are doing meaningful and sacred work. And as I have shared before, just coming to sit on the bimah on Friday nights has changed my perspectives on a day or a week, and allowed me the chance to pause and reflect. So for me, volunteering was very good for my mind and body.

Third, volunteering brings fun and fulfillment to your life. Now I can't say it was always fun, but to say this time was fulfilling is an understatement. There is so much that happens behind the scenes -

here in the office, during nighttime meetings, phone calls, zoom meetings. Most of the time, our events, programs and services come off so smoothly, but there is a lot that goes into making it all happen. And to have even been a small part of that is fulfilling on so many levels.

So on this Shabbat, let us think about these benefits of volunteering – connecting to others, being good for mind and body, and bringing fulfillment. And let us consider ways we can volunteer here at our temple and elsewhere so that we all may reap those benefits.

Shabbat Shalom

Marriage Reconsecration

It is special for me to be here tonight since my wife and I will celebrate our 25th anniversary in November. I'm blessed because after twenty five years, we have realized together that so much happiness comes from gratitude. Gratitude for our relationship, gratitude for our perseverance, gratitude for our kids and the lives they are building, gratitude for health, gratitude for loyalty, and so much more.

You don't always recognize it in the moment, and that is the real trick – finding ways to recognize something good and feel grateful for it in the present. It is so much better to not only have the memory, but also the knowledge that you were feeling gratitude in the moment. This is a real challenge for us in our busy and hectic world. A challenge I have to be reminded of frequently by my wife, and one I continue to work toward. As they say, stop and smell the roses! And so, in this moment, I can pause to tell my wife how grateful I am for her.

The genesis for tonight's comments was a few weeks ago as I was driving in my car, right after receiving the invitation for this event from the temple. And as a music so often can, a song came on the radio that completely hit the spot about what marriage reconsecration is and should be about. Not to be too cheesy, but the song lyrics are worth mentioning. Let me take you back to 1982, a beautiful duet by Eddie Rabbitt and Crystal Gayle. The song was titled, You and I, and the lyrics of the chorus say the following:

And I remember our first embrace
That smile that was on your face
The promises that we made
And now your love is my reward
And I love you even more
Than I ever did before

On this Shabbat, let us remember to be grateful for what we have, to show gratitude in the moment, and in doing so we reconsecrate not only our special anniversaries, but all of our relationships.

Shabbat Shalom

Looking Back

Our congregation lost a past president this past week. He was a real mensch and so very well respected in the medical community and here at our temple. Even from his retirement in Florida, he reached out to me on occasion over the past twenty months to offer encouragement and insight and it was great to see his continued love for our temple. Those who knew him were grateful to have done so and we will keep his memory as a blessing.

The wall directly past the lobby includes photos of all of our past presidents, dating back to the beginning of the congregation, one hundred eighty years ago. I often find myself standing before these photos and reflecting on what our temple must have been like during their tenures. What were the issues confronting them over their terms? Hiring new rabbis, strategic planning, curriculums, worship traditions, honoring the legacy of our temple while also looking forward, budgets, programming, dues, membership, and more. Some issues that perhaps seemed earth shattering and future shaping, and others that perhaps in hindsight were not as critical. Some issues specific to their era and some that we still confront today.

As President, along with our board of directors, we tackle the issues of our day and do our best to address our needs. As I look at those photos, I think about what all those past presidents and boards accomplished. I'm guessing they felt too, what we also feel today, that it is our job to be good stewards of our congregation, caring for our present and planning for our future. I'm certain we have that in common. We have those previous boards and presidents to thank for allowing us to get to this present. We may have called other times our heyday, but I feel like we are certainly enjoying a heyday now.

And so, on this Shabbat, let us take the time to stop, look at those photos, look at the dates of their tenure, imagine our temple during that time, reflect on what it took to get us here and be grateful for all we enjoy today.

Shabbat Shalom

Breathe

With Passover behind us, now it's time for a deep breath. And what a great lesson this can be – remembering to take a breath and find the renewal that a respite can provide to us. Our lives are so hectic so often, we forget to breathe. I have a reminder on my arm all the time – this bracelet that literally says "breathe". Over the past year, our Rabbi has often simply said to me, "look at your wrist," as if to say, slow down and breathe. A breath is invigorating, rejuvenating and allows us to pause, take stock, recharge and prepare ourselves for the busier times ahead.

So how do YOU manage your respites? What do you do? For me – I remind myself to pick up my guitar and play during some free time, to take a walk, or if you're like my wife and I, finally catch up on a streaming show, like Shrinking, which we finally did last weekend. If you're laughing, then you know…

So go find your quiet time. That time that allows you to pick up a new hobby or revisit an old one that you haven't been able to commit to. That time to curl up with a book. That time to call an old friend. That time that reminds us of a bygone era before so much technology.

Whatever it is for you, make time for quiet time. And Shabbat is already waiting there for you each week to provide some of that time.

On this Shabbat, let us remind ourselves of the value of quiet time, and let us remember to breathe.

Shabbat Shalom

From Suffering to Blessing

From my book of daily blessings by Rabbi Kerry Olitzky, I read this statement earlier this week: "Ultimately, we choose whether to draw on our understanding of suffering to be a blessing to others." The discussion of this quote centered on how we respond to suffering, suggesting that suffering isn't to be feared, but what is to be feared is that suffering would have no meaning, and that it is up to us to determine whether our suffering can be used as a blessing for others.

I always find it uncanny when something I read in this book

mirrors something happening in my life. And this statement was timely, because unfortunately, in the past week, I was witness to some unbearable suffering, accompanied by tremendous loss. And yet, that suffering created a massive gathering of friends and family from so many walks of life, with people crossing paths that they did not even realize were shared with many others. There was a connectivity of places, people and events, of love and emotion, all out of this suffering. It was almost as if there was a healing, and dare I say, a joy, happening at the same time as the intense suffering.

We would never wish suffering or unexpected loss on anyone, but consider how that suffering can be used to bring people together, to make them revel in memories, memories of joy and laughter and love – this week, that was the blessing.

On this Shabbat, let us hope that with any suffering, we can find our way through to blessing.

Shabbat Shalom

Significance

I'm fascinated by the night sky. Every time I look up on a clear night, I am awed, humbled, perplexed, and filled with the most sincere curiosity.

I am so fascinated that I have planned a trip this fall for Death Valley national park, which is a great place for hiking, but also doubles as a designated dark sky location in the United States. These dark sky areas have very little ambient light around them, such that the view of the night sky is full of not just a few stars, like you might see in our city night sky, but thousands of stars and galaxies, including the Milky Way, and colors beyond what you could see here in the city. I truly cannot wait. They say nothing good happens after midnight, but I think on those nights, I'll beg to differ.

Perhaps you noticed on March 28th, when, shortly after sunset, there was a very rare phenomenon where Mercury, Venus, Mars, Jupiter and Uranus were all in alignment below a newish moon. And perhaps you saw the 60 Minutes piece a few weeks ago showing images from the Webb Telescope that are mind boggling and even beyond what we can truly comprehend with regard to time and space. Our brains simply cannot grasp the distances of space. The closest star to our solar system is Proxima Centauri, which is 4.24 light years away, a distance that would take 6,300 years to travel to with current technology. Talk about feeling small and insignificant.

So why do I tell you all of this. Because I often feel that sense of smallness and insignificance when I look at the night sky and yet, I have come to peace with that feeling. And that feeling of insignificance in the universe underscores our need to find significance in our lives, on whatever piece of this earth you call home. Do you find that significance in what you mean to your family, your parents, your siblings, your children? Certainly, they don't think you are insignificant. Do you find it in your career and the positive results you bring to your job, your company, your clients, in whatever ways you help them? Do you find that significance in helping others less fortunate? That holy work is definitely significant to those in need.

And so, despite the grandeur of the night sky and how small it might make us feel, one phone call from a family member or friend, one pat on the back at work, one moment spent doing tikkun olam, can provide meaning in our lives and confirm our significance.

On this Shabbat, let us glance up at the night sky in wonder and amazement, and at the same time, remember that here on Earth, we each matter, and we are each significant.

Shabbat Shalom

Chazak

As I look back on this past year, my first thought is, "wow, how fast the time has gone by." And yet, I also find myself looking forward to the all that is left to do through the completion of my term.

We now enter the 181st year of this congregation. Let us reflect on that for just a moment. 181 years! Generations upon generations have called our temple their home. We are the beneficiaries of all that has been done before us, and yet there is more work to be done for those that will call our temple home in the future, as we forge ahead with our goal of serving the needs of all of our members, and our community.

There are traditional words said at the conclusion of reading each book of the Torah. As the last passage of a book is read, we say, Chazak, Chazak, v'nitchazeik. This translates to "Be Strong, Be Strong, and together we are strengthened." Or a more loose translation is Be Strong, Be Strong, and let us strengthen one another." As we transition to the 181st year of our congregation, and we move our congregation forward, we can say these same words because we are a strong congregation. There is power in our ability to work with one another, strengthen one another, and make a difference here at Wise Temple, and in our community.

On this Shabbat, let us say together, Chazak Chazak V'nitchazeik: Be Strong, Be Strong and let us strengthen one another, and let this be our blessing for the next year.

Shabbat Shalom

Sacred Time

Almost two full years into the job and I happened upon an article on the URJ's website titled 8 timely lessons for congregational presidents. Perhaps it would have been better had I seen this about two years ago, but alas, here we are. The lessons focus on how to manage congregational duties, how to work with rabbis and staff, developing future leadership, and how to respect the history and tradition of the congregation.

The last lesson, though, was of particular interest to me. It said to reserve a small piece of congregational life for myself. Consider what felt most sacred to me and continue to participate in that part of temple life without letting temple business intrude. I have been involved in temple business for almost fifteen years now. It's hard to remember a time when temple business didn't intrude on my participation in whatever I may be doing at temple. But I realized that there was one piece of congregational life in particular that has remained sacred to me from my pre-temple business period, and also one that I have carved out during my time as president. First, from the past, is the feeling I always have listening to the choir during the high holy days. That might sound strange coming from someone who always highlighted guitar and camp style music. But there is something about those melodies – some beautiful, some haunting, some so powerful, that have always stuck with me, not just on the holidays, but throughout the year. The time I spend listening to those melodies is sacred, and I can listen without the intrusion of other business. And the new piece of congregational life I have carved for myself is the time I spend in my chair on the bimah. I may get to sit there by virtue of my office, but this has become sacred time for me as well. I don't just watch you all from this spot. I mean, I do, but there is much more happening for me during this hour. Being in that spot has allowed me to appreciate what Shabbat is about, and allows me to pause, relax, and take a moment to breathe, often at the end of a busy week, often when I needed it most.

And so on this Shabbat, consider what are the most sacred parts of congregational life for you – the ones where the business of your daily life does not intrude and let us continue making space for these sacred moments.

Shabbat Shalom

Reflections on Two Years

When I started as President, the two year term almost seemed imposing, and yet here we are and it feels like, "where did the time go". As is typical, on a daily basis, that time can seem to go oh so slowly, but on a yearly basis, it has flown by.

This job is truly a team job. One look at our weekly email and you can see so many programs, services, community opportunities, and get a sense of how many people are needed to make this place run. It is not just our officers, or just our Board of Trustees. It is a dedicated group of our Rabbis, staff and so many volunteers that make Wise Temple a special place. A house of worship, a house of study, a community gathering space, and a place that sparks community involvement and volunteering. Being even a small part of that activity, one that works so hard for today and yet honors our past and traditions, gives such meaning to my work as President and the work of board of trustees.

As President, I received notices whenever there was a birth, engagement, marriage or death in our congregation. Watching the circle of life at our temple is thrilling, joyous, sad and humbling. We have the power to provide for so many people at all stages of life and during my term, I tried to keep in mind that I was a steward of that responsibility, one that I never took lightly. I am truly humbled by our responsiveness to the needs of our congregants.

This temple is and always has been my home. And our past presidents have always set an amazing precedent – they remain involved and engaged and I will aspire to do the same.

It has been my honor and privilege these past two years to serve the only congregation that has been part of my entire life. And I am so confident in our temple's future because our new leadership is an amazing group of people.

I have said this before, but it is appropriate here tonight – Chazak, Chazak, v'nitchazeik - From strength to strength, we are strengthened. May our congregation continue to go from strength to strength.

Shabbat Shalom

High Holy Days #1

As a lifelong member at our temple, my family's attachment to this congregation goes back more than eighty-five years. And while it is difficult for me to imagine what congregational life was like eight decades earlier, I am certain we are so different today because our temple has always been progressive in the way we think about our Judaism. This was Isaac Mayer Wise's gift to us. Rabbi Wise would not have expected the congregation to look and feel the same in every generation. He would have wanted us to adapt.

And adapt we have done: we are more than a large congregation with a diverse membership. So when we come together, we remember our shared common bond of our Reform Judaism, learning from each others' diverse viewpoints. Reform Judaism elevates informed choice – learn what you can about any topic, use your knowledge of Jewish Values as a lens through which to discern that topic, and engage in lively but civil debate. This is what we strive for now and in the years to come.

Given our diversity and willingness to adapt, it is important to consider what value our special congregation holds for us in our lives today. In our increasingly transactional lives, I suggest that our temple is a place where we can all make a contribution for the greater good.

Our membership contributions and our investment of time and energy are not just for us as individuals, but to support so many others among us- it is the very nature of what community is all about. We strengthen ourselves by strengthening one another in so many ways. Our shared resources mean that younger people provide for older members and older members provide for the needs of our youngest families as well.

When we build our congregational community, we are building and shaping the lives of others, those we know, and those we do not, those in our own cohort and those that are spread across four generations. And even more than the few thousand people that make up our temple, our membership contributions and active involvement also provide for urgent needs in our larger Cincinnati community in which we participate. And beyond Cincinnati, our congregation is internationally considered a pillar of Reform Judaism throughout the world. So together, we are contributing not only to ourselves, but to others and to building the future.

Whether you are here often or infrequently, your support is an affirmation of our mission: Specifically, our mission is this: Our sacred community cultivates deep multi-generational connections with Reform Judaism, each other, God, and the world around us through meaningful worship, lifelong Jewish learning, and acts of good deeds. Worship, Jewish Learning and Good Deeds. That is what we are about.

I encourage all of you to take part in something new this year, finding just one activity to help us fulfill that mission. In this way, you can see the value that we provide and feel proud to say you are a member of our congregation.

May this be a year of understanding, adaptation and renewed commitment to our mission.

Shanah Tovah

High Holy Days #2

As it does each year, Yom Kippur brings us to a crossroad in our lives. A crossroad between sin and repentance, between holding grudges and forgiveness, between action and inaction. In fact, the Haftorah portion for today, from the book of Isaiah, implores us to make something of our fast, to make our actions and deeds more meaningful and sacred.

And yet, at our temple, we are not only about others. Through our classes, and worship, and our spiritual offerings, we provide many opportunities to turn inward and listen carefully to the voice within. The prophet Elijah had his own inward search and in this biblical story, it is said that amidst so much noise, he heard the *still small voice*.

Those three words appear often in our liturgy, especially during these High Holy Days. In fact, right at the outset of our worship on Rosh Hashanah eve, we read the following: During the next ten days, let me face the truth about myself and listen to Your still, small voice. And then on Rosh Hashanah day, it appeared again in the Shofar service where the liturgy read: And so a great shofar will cry t'kiah. A still small voice will be heard. And it appears in many other places as well. Perhaps you have noticed some of them.

I am fascinated whenever I hear these words in our liturgy or as part of a sermon. *Still small voice.* You cannot deny the evocative nature of that phrase. How are we to define this? You can interpret this phrase many ways. For some, it may be God. For others, it may be your own conscience. For others, it may yet be something else. One commentary on this phrase says that listening to the still small voice actually means opening yourself up to a constant flow of divine energy, and that requires quieting your mind and your ego – as hard as that is to do.

So the question is – amidst all of the loudness of our world, do we take the time to listen for the still small voice that is often found within. Something from deep inside that allows us to navigate the noise and create focus.

The High Holy Days and this season of T'shuvah, of returning, help us to focus our attention and listen for that voice. We need to listen so that we may respond more fully every day. Respond to our own needs and those of our community.

Your congregation, our congregation, is here to help you do that. To add meaning to your life, through worship, learning, social action or community involvement. There is always something happening at our temple. Adult Learning offers a few classes each week. Alternative Shabbat Services, a few times a year, offer the opportunity for additional reflection and learning. Musicians in Residence offer the opportunity for Jewish music to seep into your soul and help you find your voice. And our many community action programs help you answer the call that the still small voice asks of you.

And so throughout the next year, from this High Holy Day season to the next, take some time, reflect, listen for the still small voice and act upon it here in your congregation – and may it guide you to a better year, a more fulfilling year, a year of happiness and health, a year of gratitude, a year of selflessness, a year of growth, and a year of peace.

Shanah Tovah

Made in the USA
Coppell, TX
07 December 2023

25585133R00118